"We as people are more productive, creative, committed and interconnected when we have positive emotions and thoughts about the work and when we are motivated by fundamental interest in the work itself."

Dr. Suresh Devnani

Happiness Centered Business

Igniting Principles of Growing a Sustainable Business

DR. SURESH DEVNANI

ISBN: 9781502461056

This Book is dedicated to:

My ever supportive Father, Mother, Wife and amazing Children

TABLE OF CONTENTS

INTRODUCTION

In today's economic scenario, it is more crucial than ever for businesses to have happy and productive employees. When employees are loyal and involved in a company, profits are higher, customer relationships are stronger, productivity is greater, and the company's prospects are ever growing. Equally, when people feel unmotivated or undervalued, a company deteriorates. Furthermore, multiple studies validate that employees that feel connected to their job skip less work, function better, are more supportive of changes and are generally enthusiastic to make them happen. This is because employees that feel happy are those that believe in a business, what it stands for, and as a result hope to grow with it.

Employees are to a business what gears are to any working machine, but when those gears and components don't work in unison, or resist being moved, the machine as a whole will inevitably fall apart.

But keeping employees happy is no easy task. In fact, why don't you ask yourself if you are happy? And if you aren't, you may be thinking you won't have much luck making your employees happy either. The truth is, happiness requires work from within a person.

"So, where do we find this lasting happiness? In the realization of the ultimate nature of ourselves. Everything is here within us. The truth is within us. Happiness is within us. True happiness and peace of mind cannot be found in anything external; it can only be found within."

Sogyal Rinpoche

In addition to this, there are so many other factors that contribute to a person's sense of wellbeing: friends, family and employment can all enhance or diminish from a person's sense of happiness or wellbeing. So if your workplace is stressful, where inappropriate behavior such as "back-stabbing" and gossiping is occurring, you may not evidently notice it at first, but in the long run, the productivity of your employees' will inevitably deteriorate.

Happy employees are also content employees, and feel a sense of achievement in their work. They appreciate themselves and what they do, and they find gratification from their work, believing that what they do is significant. Such emotions reduce stress, which is a major factor affecting productivity.

Happiness should be made into a competitive edge, as it shapes corporate culture, helps attract the most talented people, encourages them to work harder, and makes them stay longer. Because at the end of each financial year, any business reviewing its departmental spending will realise that their harassment lawsuits, human resources and retraining costs are ever-increasing. In this culture of lawyers and lawsuits, companies are being faced with a whole new unprecedented challenge of keeping their employees happy and content in their positions. Because when everything is considered, businesses spend an disproportionate amount of money dealing with these problems as they arise rather than investing to prevent them.

As the old proverbial saying goes, 'prevention is always better than a cure.'

I have arrived at the following key elements that businesses need to practice in order to create the happiness centered businesses blueprint of the 21st century:

1. Purpose comes before profit.

2. A company and its employees are partners.

3. A cooperative organisation.

4. Value-based leadership.

Through experience and working with my own companies, I have come to realize that people often forget, and sometimes don't know, how to be happy when they're working. This book provides essential guidelines that can make work fun, inspiring and energizing, and includes great advice and tools on how to deal with workplace conflict to avoid stress and burnout.

Multiple research has confirmed that successful companies are not those purely based on financial gains but are those running on positive corporate and social responsibilities.

The level of employee engagement, warmth and sense of shared purpose is tangible. While my conclusion may be partial, there are numerous studies and reports confirming that happy employees lead directly to better performance and higher profits.

Happiness Centered Businesses are the future, and will eventually come to all workplaces. Some of todays most well-known business models that have grown from start-ups into billion dollar companies both understand and believe in the principle that in order for a company to grow, its employees must be happy and grow with it. The infamous example of Google is a true model of a corporation employing the techniques of keeping its employees happy to offer a great and effective product. Following in this example, there is a massive tendency in the business world to focus more and more on making work a happy experience, and this is coming to your country, and your company soon.

The reason behind it is simple yet empowering: today, customer service, efficiency and innovation are key to any organisation's success. It does not matter how efficient a company is, what is important is that it can creatively invent tomorrow. Nobody cares how efficient its business processes are if it cannot provide a satisfactory experience to its customers.

The Customer is King.

"Happy employees are more creative, provide better service and work more efficiently. Businesses often forget about the culture, and ultimately, they suffer for it because you can't deliver good service from unhappy employees."

Tony Hsieh

1

BRING ON THE HAPPINESS AND RING IN THE PROFITS

Productivity measures across national economies have captivated the attention of policy makers and executives alike. According to John Helliwell, Professor Emeritus and an economist from **The University of British Columbia** presented research on happiness and well-being, based on surveys of more than 100,000 people in Canada and around the world. Among his findings, which have significant implications for the workplace, is that a slight positive increase in a worker's relationship with the boss may translate into a substantial increase in compensation or productivity. [1]Ultimately, the source of productivity is the individual knowledge of workers who get things done every day. And the evidence is clear: People perform better when they're happier.

There has been extensive research focused on creativity, productivity, and the psychology of everyday work life. Whether pointed at entrepreneurial startups or large MNC's, the same holds true: People are more productive and creative when they have more positive emotions. In fact, we found that, if an employee is happier on a given day, they were not only more likely to come up with a new idea or solve a complex problem that same day, but also to do so the next day. The one big problem is that although this may be known to the vast majority of business owners and managers they often overlook the

---

[1] "How Workplace Happiness Can Boost Productivity." *Psychology Today: Health, Help, Happiness + Find a Therapist.* N.p., n.d. Web. 14 May 2014.

potential of this proposition. Most individuals fail to consider the wider ramifications of these benefits, such as their employees feeling less stressed, working harder, displaying a larger degree of loyalty and pride in their work, which overall, contributes to the success of the company. These benefits are often overlooked because to the majority of us, we recognise their impact as being insignificant. But the truth is, any successful business owner or entrepreneur will likely confess that it is as the result of the collective efforts of their employees that they attribute the success of their business.

To grasp this concept, a business can be seen as a military ship sailing in a sea, where a business owner or manager is the captain. The most fundamental error the captain can make on any voyage or mission is to fallaciously believe that he or she is the sole factor affecting whether or not the ship is successful in carrying out its task. It is only when the captain understands the necessity of each and every crewmember, whether controlling the navigation or manning the engines, that he or she may truly sail their ship effectively. Although, if the captain had an unhappy crew, while it may not be noticeable at first, the ship will indefinitely sink, and in the time being, will not run at its true capacity. When crewmembers are looking to defect and constantly spend their time and effort considering moving to other ships and other vocations as a whole, the vessel as a whole suffers. But consider the alternative, when each crewmember defends the ship and carries out their task with pride and loyalty. The efforts of the crew that would have been channeled outwards looking for alternative prospects, are now being channeled inwards, and all of a sudden, collectively, the vessel as a whole prospers.

Economists have established a link between workers' happiness and their performance, and repeatedly note that employers should recognize the relationship.

Research conducted by a team led by Andrew Oswald, a professor of economics at Warwick Business School, states, "Happy workers are 12 per cent more productive than the average employee while unhappy workers are 10 per cent less."

Gallup measured the link between employees' feelings and corporate outcomes, reporting that lost productivity due to employee disengagement costs more than $300 billion in the U.S. annually. Another separate conducted by Dr. James Harter and his colleagues found that business unit sales and profits at any given point in time can be predicted by employees' feelings about the organization at earlier points in time.[2]

---

[2] Amabile, Teresa, and Steven Kramer. *Bloomberg Business Week*. Bloomberg, n.d. Web. 14 May 2014.

Organizations need to keep their employees happy. As suggested by Jill Geisler In her book, Work Happy: What Great Bosses Know, she suggests four measures: a supervisor who cares (happy employees believe their boss listens to them and actually takes their input seriously); sincere, specific praise and feedback; supportive and fair workplace culture; ways to put new employees off on the right foot.[3]

Geisler further adds in her book that hiring well is also a part of the equation. She suggests that organizations should look for people who are positive in nature, hard working, and those that will add to the team.

In the fight for competitive advantage where employees are the differentiator, creating an environment where employees feel happy to be associated with the organization should be the ultimate goal.

In Business...

A 1% increase (very modest) in productivity would bring a benefit of $400 per employee per year, based on the national average salary of $40,000 assuming 40% overheads.

A company with just 50 employees would realize a benefit of $20,000 annually.

---

[3] Kashyap, Gyanendra K. "Around the World." *HR Pro* ::. N.p., 25 Jan. 2013. Web. 14 May 2014.

A company with 5,000 employees would realize a benefit of $2,000,000 annually.

Happy people are healthier than unhappy people. A reduction in sickness absence by just 1 day per year per employee would bring a benefit of $167.00 based on the national average salary of $40,000 assuming 240 working days.

A company with just 50 employees would realize a benefit of $8,333 annually.

A company with 5,000 employees would realize a benefit of $833,333 annually.

Happier employees don't quit the company as often, especially when supported by a culture of 'happiness in the workplace'. A mere 10% reduction in turnover would bring a benefit of $256 based on the assumption that the cost of recruiting, training and covering someone leaving is approximately equivalent to 40% of their annual salary – here taken to be $40,000.

A company with just 50 employees would realize a benefit of $12,800 annually.

A company with 5,000 employees would realize a benefit of $1,280,000 annually.

Total annual benefit realized for a company with just 50 employees: $41,133.

Total annual benefit realized for a company with 5,000 employees: $4,113,333.

"Our truest life is when we are in dreams awake."

Henry David Thoreau

2

THE MONDAY BLUES

Have you ever experienced the Monday morning blues? Monday morning blues are not just a naturally occurring phenomenon that all of us experience, but a symptom of a greater problem. In fact, the problem is that most people dismiss their Monday morning experience as one of the burdens of life, and never realize that there is a way to overcome it. When we consider the first working day of the week (Monday) juxtaposed against the relaxation we had experienced over the weekend, it is hard to believe that this can be cured. But the truth is that it definitely can. The Monday morning blues are a symptom of a much greater problem, the problem of feeling overwhelmed, stressed, or just bored of your work.

As a purely unscientific study based on my personal experience interacting with hundreds of individuals at dozens of companies, I would estimate that about 5 to 10% of people at any given company truly love their work. Keep in mind; most people will never admit to even themselves that they aren't passionate about their work. They could be in denial about it, be completely unaware that something better exists, or have convinced themselves that where they are is perfect because admitting otherwise would mean they would have to change. But if you get to know someone well enough, this embarrassing truth will often will come out.

Occasionally, I ask people, if they love their

work? It is seldom the answer is yes, more than ever if I asked this question on a Friday or Saturday.

I am not saying 90% of people hate their job. I am saying that 90% or more of people aren't passionate about their work. And as I discussed earlier, this astonishing figure can be a time bomb waiting to happen.

But there are always those rare individuals that cannot stop bubbling about their exciting projects and are truly inspiring in their dedication and passion. But the majority of people, when asked this question, have their eyes dropped to the ground for just an instant.

You too can discover a job you love. For most, it won't be a magical discovery that suddenly hits you. It's an ongoing process in life of noticing when you are having the most fun, and starting to incorporate those experiences into your work. Of course, this is much easier to do if you are self-employed.

In simple words, if you love your job and are passionate about what you are doing, going to work on Monday morning is another opportunity to do what you love. It is always a challenge to start another seemingly endless workweek if you are feeling under appreciated or are unsatisfied with your job. And if this is the case, looking ahead at another 10, 20 or 30 years here, depending on how old you are can seem as daunting as any task you have ever faced before.

ACTION PLAN FOR HAPPY WEEK

Following list of simple actions will help in beating the blues, and allow you to greet the new week like it's Friday night.

1. **Don't live for the weekends.** Multiple studies have shown people who are stressed at work tend to be much happier on the weekend. So don't only look forward to Saturday and Sunday; try to spread out the joy and plan something fun during the week, like a movie night with pals on a weekday night. In addition to this, organise an event with your family that you agree to do on a weekday, and establish a routine. Something as small as Pizza nights at home or eating dinner out with your children can help brighten up your week.

2. **Relax.** Pick either Friday or Saturday night to go out, and spend another evening staying home with friends. Too much time out and about may lead to less sleep and nasty hangovers which are really felt on Monday mornings.

3. **Don't sleep in**. Who can resist sleeping till noon? But instead of waking up just in time for lunch, try sticking to the usual sleeping pattern all week to feel rested and energized all week long.

4. **Plan ahead on Sunday night.** Lay out the Monday morning outfit and pack a good lunch the night before— eliminating any stress in the morning will only make Monday's more tolerable. Make a check-list, put up sticky notes or set a reminder on your phone, anything that will take the burden off your mind of remembering. And remember to re-set the alarm in order to wake up on time and avoid being late for work.

5. **Hit the hay early on Sunday.** Make sure to get around 7 hours of sleep to gear up for the workweek. Getting to bed at a reasonable hour will make the alarm clock our new friend.

6. **Don't skip breakfast**. We need the boosted metabolism to jump-start the day with an energy boost.

7. **Get pumped with some tunes.** While getting ready for work, turn up the stereo (or Pandora). Listening to music can enhance your mood and get us pumped for work.

8. **Hit the early morning gym.** It's no secret that exercises amps up endorphin levels; so try getting in early morning exercise to start the day off right.

9. **Dress up.** New dress, new day. Save that latest fun purchase for Monday morning, or even something bright to feel more confident when headed to the office. Dress to impress, if you look good, you're likely to feel good.

10. **Smile!** Smile in the shower, flash that smile at the barista, and show those pearly whites to the whole office. Studies show that when you smile long enough, the

11. **Take small breaks throughout the day**. Don't stay glued to the cubicle all day. Take a walk to get some fresh air, avoid eating lunch at your desk, or go to the gym for a quick workout. But most important of all, schedule these breaks so that you know exactly when you're going, and how long you can take without feeling guilty.

12. **Make a list of 10 things you are grateful for.** Starting the week out with gratitude, taking the time in recognising and appreciating the things that you enjoy about work. These don't have to be big things, but even the little things like being grateful for the weather, or that you got to kiss your wife good-morning.

13. **List all the things that excited.** Most of us look at the week ahead of us and think of all the tough stuff we have to do and the difficult tasks ahead of us. On Sunday make a list of at least three things that you are looking forward to. A new day is a new opportunity.

14. **Help others to feel happy.** Do something nice for someone else as soon as you get to work on Monday will definitely lift the

spirits, and actually help shift the overall mood in your work space.

"Obstacles cannot crush me. Every obstacle yields to stern resolve. He who is fixed to a star does not change his mind.'

Leonardo da Vinci

3

HAPPY OFFICE DESIGN

Want to inject a bit more enthusiasm into your workers? Zing up your surroundings and start reaping the benefits with our guide to creating the best environment for your office.

Having a well-designed office isn't just about looking slick in the eyes of prospective clients and customers. Creating the best possible working environment also helps cultivate a workforce that is motivated, happy, engaged and effective.

Gone are the days of harsh lighting and bare walls. Office spaces are transforming into hubs of creativity, contributing towards an employee's attitude and performance. After all, this is a place where many of us spend a very sizeable portion of our lives – so it's no surprise the office environment makes a huge difference to how we feel about our roles and our work.

With so much time being spent at the office, if our employees are not happy being there, it can make them dread Monday mornings and watch the clock eagerly awaiting the end of the workday. Equally, if they enjoy being at work and find the atmosphere agreeable and comfortable, they will likely work harder and not be in such a rush to run out on the dot at 5p.m. And don't forget, happier employees are more productive - and productivity ties directly to profits.

As an owner of multiple businesses, I have come to realize that physical environment can serve as a foundation for effective work output.

Various studies have come to the conclusion that the power of choice and autonomy to drive not only employee happiness, but also motivation and performance. is when companies allow them to help decide when, where, and how they work. These employees were more likely to be satisfied with their jobs, performed better, and viewed their company as more innovative than competitors that didn't offer such choices.

As further suggested by Dr. Craig Knight in his extensive research, "When people feel uncomfortable in their surroundings they are less engaged – not only with the space but also with what they do in it. If they can have some control, that all changes and people report being happier at work, identifying more with their employer, and are more efficient when doing their jobs."[4]

Results have constantly confirmed the proposition that the more control people have over their office spaces, the happier and more motivated they were in their jobs. They felt physically more comfortable at work, identified more with their employers, and felt more positive about their jobs in general.

---

[4] Knight, C.P., & Haslam, S.A. (2010). Your Place or Mine? Organizational Identification and Comfort as Mediators of Relationships Between the Managerial Control of Workspace and Employees' Satisfaction and Well-being. British Journal of Management, 21, 717-735.

Summary thus far:

- **Make your office a space that your employees want to be in**
- **Give your employees the paint brush**
- **Give your team the means to be creative**
- **Do away with the traditional layout**
- **Create a buzz**

At their headquarters Facebook employees have the ability to tailor the layout, height, and configuration of their own desks based on personal preference. Teams are also allowed to create workspace that best supports their project. Besides this, there are also a number of meeting spaces spread

across the campus available to all employees. Facebook also offers a range of options to employees for managing their personal lives and time, ranging from the transactional (banks, cleaners) to social (restaurants, arcades) and those services that lie somewhere in between (woodshop, studio). This has proven to lead to greater organizational productivity and suggests that meeting an employee's need for autonomy can influence motivation and performance.

Not every company can offer choice to employees on the same scale. But all organizations should carefully consider what they could do to give employees the spaces and tools that enhance and support their workday tasks as well as corporate goals. Choice is not a one-size-fits-all approach. Rather, it's specific to the organization and its needs.

Encourage Staff to Make Their Space Their Own - allow employees to extensively personalize their own workspace.

Break Down the Walls – Allow open workspaces that make it easier to collaborate and create a rejuvenated and open environment.

Establish a Balanced Space - Open and designate space for collaboration, but balance is critical. The four work modes that need to be considered: focus, collaboration, learning and socializing. Dedicated quiet spaces for research and learning, an area to socialize and relax, an area for collaboration and spontaneous meetings as well as semi-private space to allow for quiet and concentration are all key to this.

Organize **Social Activities -** Socializing between employees is a key motivator. Having dedicated social spaces that include a pool table, tabletop space to sit and chat, gourmet coffee or snacks. If company has a modest budget then they should have a den-like area with a sofa and table and chairs can allow workers to sit and visit over lunch or coffee.

Worker retention is critical to saving money on expenses associated with turnover.

On the other hand improved worker engagement can encourage efficiency, productivity and performance – all of which can improve your company's bottom line. Making the workplace happier is a great way to make your employees happier.

"We must become the change we want to see.'

Mahatma Gandhi

4

HAPPY WORK
MEDITATION

Meditation has been shown to produce a wide range of mental benefits when practiced on a daily basis. Studies have shown that it can actually change how the brain processes information and manages the effects of stress, depression, and anxiety. Those who practice meditation at least once a day, research has demonstrated, are happier and calmer than their counterparts who don't, so it's no surprise that many high-stress businesses are catching on and making meditation a part of their corporate mission.

Meditation went mainstream at healthcare benefits company, Aetna, some time ago. The company even took part in clinical trials using mindfulness and yoga (Viniyoga) workplace programs, to help individual's better deal with stress at work.

At the Wisdom 2.0 Business Conference in New York City this fall, Aetna's CEO Mark Bertolini spoke very openly about how these programs reduced "perceived stress" and "stress levels" in participants. And, how the programs have been a crucial part of the companies edict to value talent.

"We really need to redefine health as keeping people healthy so they're more productive, if their more productive they're more economically viable, if they're economically viable, they are happier," says Bertolini who goes onto say when workers are happier, they can better contribute to their communities within an organization.

Mindfulness practice has been linked to activating parts of the brain correlated with constructs of well being such as happiness, joy and enhanced self-awareness.

One of the best -- and cheapest -- ways to become healthier and happier is through meditation exercises. Just after nine weeks of training, participants from our meditation program had "an increased sense of purpose and had fewer feelings of isolation and alienation. The effects of stress reduction techniques are equally dramatic on our productivity, creativity, energy and performance.

It's not just the number of hours one sits at a desk that determines the value one generates. It's the final output that is released that matters. Maintaining a steady reservoir of energy -- physically, mentally, emotionally and even spiritually -- requires refueling it intermittently.

In a nutshell, happiness and productivity are not only related, they are correlated.

According to the iOpener Institute, a company with 1,000 employees, increasing happiness (those less stressed, connected to their jobs and much more) in the workplace[5]:

- Reduces the cost of employee turnover by 46%

- Reduces the cost of sick leave by 19%

- Increases performance and productivity by 12%

And the happiest employees spend 40% more time focused on tasks and feel energized 65% more of the time. Happier employees also take six fewer sick days a year, and remain in their jobs twice as long.

This is why more and more companies are realizing that their employees' health is one of the most important predictors of the company's health.

Google is one company that "gets it," and offers employees an internal health rejuvenation program named S.I.Y., short for "Search Inside Yourself." It was started by Chade-Meng Tan, engineer, Google employee number 107, and the author of *Search Inside Yourself: The Unexpected Path to Achieving Success, Happiness (and World Peace)*. The course has three parts: attention training, self-knowledge, and building useful mental habits.

---

[5] Huffington, Arianna. "Mindfulness, Meditation, Wellness and Their Connection to Corporate America's Bottom Line." *The Huffington Post*. TheHuffingtonPost.com, 18 Mar. 2013. Web. 14 May 2014.

"The main business case for meditation is that if you're fully present on the job, you will be more

effective as a leader," says William George, Harvard Business School professor, former CEO of Medtronic, and a guest on Tuesday's show. "You will make better decisions."6

"There is no work-life balance," says Janice Marturano. "We have one life. What's most important is that you be awake for it."6

---

6 "From the Front Lines." *Leader to Leader Journal.* N.p., 2012. Web. 14 May 2014.

'Neither fire nor wind, birth nor death can erase our good deeds.'

Buddha

5

WELL-BEING TO HAPPINESS

The five paths to well-being and happiness are based on a set of positive actions that have been developed to help get people started on their way to a happier life. While we all have different circumstances and different likes and dislikes, these five ways are broad enough for you to find your own style of happiness. Try them out at work and in your daily life and see how well they work for you.

CONNECT: With the people around you. With family, friends, colleagues and neighbors. At home, work, and within local community, think of these elements as the cornerstones of your life and invest time in developing them. Building these connections will support and enrich you every day.

BE ACTIVE: Go for a walk or run. Step outside. Cycle. Play a game. Garden. Dance. Exercise releases endorphins which makes you feel good. and gives you an overall sense of control and well-being. Most importantly, discover a physical activity that you enjoy and one that suits your level of mobility and fitness.

TAKE NOTICE: Be curious. Catch sight of the beautiful. Embark on the unusual. Notice the changing seasons. Savor the moment, whether you are walking to work, eating lunch or talking to friends. Be aware of the world around you and what you are feeling. Reflecting on your experiences will help you appreciate what matters to you.

KEEP LEARNING: Try something new. Rediscover an old interest. Sign up for that course you have been thinking of. Take on a different responsibility at work. Fix a bike. Learn to play an instrument or how to cook your favorite food. Set a challenge you will enjoy achieving. Learning new things will make you more confident as well as being fun.

GIVE: Do something nice for a friend, or a stranger. Thank someone. Smile. Volunteer your time. Join a community group. Look out, as well as in. Seeing yourself, and your happiness, linked to the wider community can be incredibly rewarding and creates connections with the people around you.

EPILOGUE

Many people I have worked with feel that if they become successful at work, they will automatically become happy. But in reality, this scenario is in fact reversed. It's important to become happy, which will then help you become successful.

It is crucial for organizations to allow their employees to be happy, and not just for the employees themselves. "The greatest competitive advantage in the modern economy is a positive and engaged workforce."

"Without it, happiness can create irrational optimists." Shawn Achor, founder and CEO of Good Think, Inc., suggests that what is needed is the cultivation of "rational optimism." The latter "requires taking a realistic assessment of the present, both the bad and the good, while maintaining a belief that our behavior matters. Rose-colored glasses will not help, but an optimistic brain will help your team overcome the biggest challenges."

People can also help fulfill their potential by better understanding the role of social support at work. The key to remember is that giving support is even better than receiving it. "In an era of do-more-with-less," "we need to stop lamenting how little social support we feel from managers, coworkers and friends, and start focusing our brain's own resources on how we can increase the amount of social support we provide to the people in our lives. The greatest predictor of success and happiness at work is social support. And the greatest way to increase social support is to provide it to others."

"In the working world," he says, "working with leaders, I began to discover that some of the same principles that caused Harvard students to rise to the top were also the same principles used by leaders to become more successful. Those seven research principles became the basis for *The Happiness Advantage*." Closely related to happiness is the concept of thriving. Gretchen Spreitzer, a professor at the University of Michigan's Ross School of Business, and her coauthors delineate this concept in their paper "Thriving at Work: Toward Its Measurement, Construct Validation, and Theoretical Refinement," published in the *Journal of Organizational Behavior*.

"Thriving is like happiness in that it also involves the experience of positive emotions," Spreitzer says. "But it is focused on a specific type of positive emotion—what we term as vitality or energy. When people are thriving in their work, they feel alive at work. Their work is literally fueling them with energy. But thriving means a lot more than just feeling positive emotions. It also includes a sense that one is growing, learning or getting better at what they are doing. This suggests that thriving is about making progress or having positive momentum rather than languishing or feeling stunted."

Everyone at work can consciously help himself or herself to thrive more. Some basic strategies involve managing energy by sleeping well, eating a balanced diet that includes frequent high-protein snacks, and taking breaks, ideally every 90 minutes. But Spreitzer and her colleagues also found that the way people engaged in their work had an effect on how well they thrived. "When individuals engage their work in a way that helps others, learn new things, and find meaning in their work, they report higher levels of thriving," she says. "So the challenge is for individuals to find ways to craft their work so they have more relational connections, more chances to try new things, and can see more of the impact in what they do."

This study suggests that leaders can create the kind of workplaces that can help people thrive. Spreitzer says, "Leaders can (1) provide their people with more opportunities for decision making discretion, (2) share more information about the organization, its strategy, and competitors, (3) set out and reinforce norms that promote civil and respectful behavior, and (4) offer performance feedback, especially about what is going well. When leaders create workplaces with these characteristics, their people feel like they can grow, develop, and thrive in their work."

Fully engaged, thriving employees finish the day not depleted but Spreitzer contends, "with energy for their family life, hobbies, and community service."

ROI OF HAPPINESS TRAINING

There are many personal and professional benefits of happiness training, not the least of which is happiness itself.

Here are some of the benefits of living a happy life and supporting happiness in the workplace with happiness training.

Happier employees don't quit the company as often, especially when supported by a culture of 'happiness in the workplace'.

EMPOWERING EMPLOYEES TO PARTICIPATE IN PERSONAL DEVELOPMENT TRAINING PAYS OFF

Every employee that took the course found it useful, and one even said it afforded her the opportunity to feel as though she could take care of 'that' part of her life, which ultimately gave her greater energy to focus on her workday.

HAPPIER EMPLOYEES ARE MORE PRODUCTIVE EMPLOYEES

A lot of interesting things started to happen toward the end of the course (and shortly thereafter), with employees really stretching themselves and going beyond the call of duty. For example, one employee took it upon herself to launch a media tools training initiative aimed at junior-level staff; another was promoted to head up an entire department.

HAPPINESS IS CONTAGIOUS

A few weeks into the class, we started getting calls and emails from other employees asking how they could sign up, or whether we were planning a follow-up course. It seems that the happiness bug was infectious, and others wanted to learn how they, too, could gain a new perspective on how to be happy. We are, in fact, launching the course with a new crop of employees this spring.

HAPPINESS INSPIRES GOOD MANAGEMENT

One of the topics discussed in the class was nurturing and how this can translate into better work and personal relationships. One participant who was having a hard time connecting with junior team members, and according to the people she manages, has made significant strides since completing the course to become more open, communicative, collaborative, and, ultimately, nurturing.

HAPPIER EMPLOYEES ARE BETTER EQUIPPED TO MANAGE STRESS

There's no denying that the advertising and media business can be stressful. Meeting client deadlines, expectations, and budgets, not to mention managing teams and trying to find your center of gravity, can be a lot to juggle. We found that by equipping employees with mechanisms and tools to tap into their "happy" sides, they can simultaneously balance workplace pressures more effectively.

The real question is:

What is it costing you and your company to NOT get happiness training?

ADDITIONAL RESCOURCES

Abuhamdeh, S., Csikszentmihalyi, M. Istanbul The importance of challenge for the enjoyment of intrinsically motivated, goal-directed activities. Sehir University, Istanbul, Turkey. Personality and Social Psychology Bulletin. 2012 March;38(3):317-30.

Amabile, T.M. & Kramer, S.J. (2012) How leaders kill meaning at work. **McKinsey Quarterly, January 2012.**

Amabile, T. M. & Kramer, S. J. (2011). The power of small wins. *Harvard Business Review*, **89 (5), 70-80.**

Amabile, Teresa; Kramer Steven. "Bring on the Smiles, Count the Profits", *The Progress Principle*

Amabile, T. M. & Kramer, S. J. (2010) What really motivates workers (#1 in breakthrough ideas for 2010). *Harvard Business Review*, **88:1, 44-45**

Amabile, T.M., Schatzel, E.A., Moneta, G.B., and Kramer, S.J. (2004). Leader behaviors and the work environment for creativity: Perceived leader support. *The Leadership Quarterly*, **15:1, 5-32.**

Amabile, T.M., and Kramer, S.J. (2007). Inner work life: Understanding the subtext of business performance.*Harvard Business Review*, **85:5, 72-83.**

Amabile, T.M., Barsade, S.G., Mueller, J.S., and Staw, B.M (2005). Affect and creativity at work.*Administrative Science Quarterly*, **50:3, 367-403.**

Amabile, T.M. (1997). Motivating creativity in organizations: On doing what you love and loving what you do.*California Management Review*, **40, 39-58.**

Bargh, J.A., Shalev, I. The substitutability of physical and social warmth in every day life. Department of Psychology, Yale University, New Haven, CT. Emotion, 2012 Feb;12(1):154-62.

Boehm, Julia, K.; Lyubomirsky, Sonja. "Does Happiness Promote Career Success?" *University of California, Riverside*

Boehm, J., Kubzansky, L. (2012), The Heart's Content: The Association Between Positive Psychological Well-Being and Cardiovascular Health, Psychological Bulletin

Boston Consulting Group. "From Capability to Profitability; Realizing the Value of People Management." 2012

Brueller, Daphna, Carmeli, Abraham, Dutton, Jane, E. (2009) Learning Behaviours in the Workplace: The Role of High-quality Interpersonal Relationships and Psychological Safety. Systems Research and Behavioral Science.

Cohen, S et al (2006), Positive Emotional Style Predicts Resistance to Illness After Experimental Exposure to Rhinovirus or Influenza, Psychosomatic Medicine

Deci, E., Ryan, R. (2008), Self-Determination Theory: A Macrotheory of Human Motivation, Development, and Health, Canadian Psychology

Diener, E., Chan, M.Y. (2011), Happy People Live Longer: Subjective Well-Being Contributes to Health and Longevity, Applied Psychology: Health and Wellbeing

Edmans, A (2011), Does the stock market fully value intangibles? Employee satisfaction and equity prices, Journal of Financial Economics

Evans, G.W., Johnson, D. Stress and open-office noise. Department of Design and Environmental Analysis, Cornell University, Ithaca, New York. Journal of Applied Psychology. 2000 Oct;85(5):779-83.

Forcier, K., Stroud, L.R., Papandonatos, G.D., et al. Links between physical fitness and cardiovascular reactivity and recovery to psychological stressors: A meta-analysis. Centers for Behavioral and Preventitive Medicine, Brown Medical School, Providence, RI. Health Psychology. 2006 November;25(6):723-39.

Heathfield, Susan M.."Are Your Employees Happy at Work?" About.com Guide August 5, 2012

J.H. Fowler and N.A. Christakis, Dynamic spread of happiness in a large social network: longitudinal analysis over 20 years, British Medical Journal, December 2008

Judge, T.A., Heller, D., Mount, M.K. Five-factor model of personality and job satisfaction: a meta-analysis. Department of Management, Warrington College of Business, University of Florida, Gainesville. Journal of Applied Psychology. 2002 Jun;87(3):530-41.

Mercer (2011), "What's Working" survey

Oswald, A.J., Proto, E., Sgroi, D (2009), Happiness and Productivity, Institute for the Study of Labor (IZA)

Pink, D. (2009), Drive: The Surprising Truth About What Motivates Us. Riverhead.

Toekr, S., Biron, M. Job burnout and depression: unraveling their temporal relationship and considering the role of physical activity. Faculty of Management, Tel Aviv University, Israel. Journal of Applied Psychology. 2012 May;97(3):699-710.

Towers and Watson. "The Power of Three; Taking Engagement to New Heights." Perspectives. 2012

www.ingramcontent.com/pod-product-compliance
Lightning Source LLC
Chambersburg PA
CBHW051246170526
45165CB00004B/1592